# Yes, Love, Thank You

Meditative Prayers and Pictures to Blossom Your Heart

# Yes, Love, Thank You

## Meditative Prayers and Pictures to Blossom Your Heart

David Long-Higgins

Yes, Love, Thank You
Meditative Prayers and Pictures to Blossom Your Heart

ISBN: 9798300895174
Printed in the USA by David Long-Higgins

For more information contact the author at
davelonghiggins@gmail.com or scan the QR code below

# Dedication

To my beloved Beth, celebrating 40 years of marriage and counting, with heartfelt thanks for the many ways you teach me about love.

"God is love."

*1 John 4:8a*

# Contents

## Love

## Thank You

## Afterword

# Acknowledgements

No book truly comes from one person, even if the original writing seems to have arisen that way.  This book is no exception as it received much helpful refinement from others whose eyes and hearts helped me see things I was not able to see, having grown too close to the words and the pictures.  Their suggestions for improvement were also accompanied by encouragement for me to keep on birthing this volume that is in your hands.  At risk of leaving someone out (my apologies in advance for that) I want to thank these dear friends without whom this collection would be diminished in all kinds of important ways.  They include Chad Abbott, Sheldon Culver, Cassidy Hall, Chris Harnden, Barbara Hubbell, Cindi Beth Johnson, Alejandro Rodriguez, Kim Sadler, and my daughter, Hannah Long-Higgins.  For all of you, I am so very grateful.

DMLH
November 2024

# The Invitation

Dear Friend,

It may seem odd to open a book with such an intimate greeting. Yet, if you have picked up this book either out of curiosity or because it has been given to you as a gift, there may just be some hunger of the heart or some yearning of spirit that has called us together. Through the prayers and photographs that follow, I hope you will discover beneath the ordinary routines and demands of life, an unnameable Presence that calls from the depths of your being. If you have noticed this at all in your life journey, you have experienced what the ancients referred to as the call to contemplative prayer. My invitation and encouragement to you is to be available to whatever urge of Spirit may be rising in you. It is this sacred nudge that joins us to one another, though we may never have the opportunity to meet. It is also an opening to that which has the power to heal, bless, and give rise to our highest joy.

## A Word about Language

The prayers in this collection are offered as portals of discovery for you to grow in your awareness of a Holy Presence saturating life that is deeper than our ability to describe or name. In this collection sometimes I have used the word "God" to address this Presence. Often, however, the words "O Love" seem to better describe the intimate presence and desire of this One who is closer to us than breathing, yet larger than we can imagine. Our deepest encounter with this Presence is often realized through loving surrender or consent to be open to the One who is Love. In this way the greatest commandments of Judaism and Christianity, to fully love God and neighbor, are more of a plea than something burdensome from the Holy One who holds and is Life.

What matters most is that you use whatever language for this Presence is helpful to you. Love will draw you in with whatever language is best for you in any given season. Though I am Christian and some of the prayers draw on the language and rhythms of the way of Jesus, I truly hope you will not let that be a stumbling block if that is not your spiritual or religious tradition or if you do not feel as though you "fit" within any one tradition or any tradition at all. Reframe the language or skip to prayers less explicitly Christian if that would be helpful to you. I simply encourage you to be open to whatever way the Presence of Love nudges you and opens you up. In this way meditation and prayer often gift one with a holy surprise.

## A Word about the Prayer Form

The form of these prayers has arisen in a way quite surprising to me. They may be read in several different ways: either in their entirety, stanza by stanza, or savored line by line in more of a lectio divina way of praying. Those familiar with the practice of Lectio Divina (divine reading) will remember that sometimes just a few words are all the soul needs to be opened to an awareness of deep Presence. Such few words may become a mantra for the day, carrying the word from head to heart, cultivating a sense of the divine in and through the ordinary. There is no one right way to engage these offerings. My only hope is that they may be helpful in nurturing your encounter with Divine Love. A brief description of Lectio Divina is included in the Afterward, should you be interested in learning more about that prayer practice.

The most important encouragement I can offer is to go slowly, lingering with a prayer or photograph for a day or a week or however long your soul needs. These prayers are not intended to be read through in a rush to other things. They are offered to slow you into an awareness of deep Presence, however that may arise for you. The counsel of mystics and contemplatives of all traditions is that Love calls us to a necessary alternative pace. In an age of information overdrive, we are invited to downshift so that we may be formed by a different rhythm and from a different place. Prayer and meditation are not finally about gaining information or forming propositions about God or the Holy. They are engagements of encounter with the alive presence of Love that can shape us deeply and differently for action in the life of the world. Given space and time, Love can and does change us from the inside out.

## A Word about the Photographs

Sometimes language in any form can be a stumbling block to an encounter with Holy Love. In such times, the visual can provide a necessary opening to this always-present Presence. Honoring what St. Francis once shared about nature being God's first bible,

I have offered an accompanying photograph for each prayer, often captured in nature. The pictures dance with the words but may be used in their own right as portals into the soul's beckoning silence. These sights have presented themselves to me from a number of places where I have been privileged to travel. I hope they may open you to the mysteries close at hand around you, wherever life may take you. You may even discover nature calling you to take your own pictures, engaging a practice called Visio Divina (divine seeing). A brief description of Visio Divina is included in the Afterward.

## A Word about the Grouping of the Prayers and Photographs

You will find the prayers and photos grouped into three sections: Yes, Love, and Thank You. Each section is offered as a reminder of Love's affirmation, desire, and call. There is no particular order these prayers and photos are intended to be used. I encourage you to simply let your holy curiosity or heart-hunger lead you. If a particular prayer or picture speaks, linger with it a while. If it doesn't speak, move on to another. Rest as little or long as your heart tells you is helpful. These are offered as portals to discover the prayer that already resides in you.

Finally, know that I hold you in prayer, though we may never meet. We are already joined by the One who is Life. The practices of meditation and prayer allow us to savor this reality more and more. It is the foundation for loving and just action in the world. Blessings on you and may the world be blessed by our sharing in this holy invitation from the One who is Love.

Grace and peace,

David Long-Higgins
November 2024

Yes

There is a Holy "Yes"
Answering the world's "no"
Pleading for our consent...

**Yes, Love, thank you,**
For raising from rest
A body renewed.

**Yes, Love, thank you,**
For the cup that holds
The renewing sip
Of Your life-giving water.

**Yes, Love, thank you,**
For scripture's gift
Carrying ancient voices
To guide my present path.

**Yes, Love, thank you,**
For silences unnameable
Sorting out my soul.

**Yes, Love, thank you,**
For lenses bringing focus
To Your world of beauty.

**Yes, Love, thank you,**
For challenging things
Strengthening my capacity
And ability to truly love.

**Yes, Love, thank you,**
For Your presence
Joining me to everything
And everyone, everywhere
Without exception.

**Yes, Love, thank you,**
For the gift of work
Inviting me to use
The many gifts given
By You for building up
A world often torn down.

**Yes, Love, thank you,**
For each breath
Of Your sustaining Spirit
Stretching heart and lung
Bearing life again and again.

**Yes, Love, thank you,**
For continually pouring
Your anointing presence
Of Christ-love
Into the world
And even into me.

**Yes, Love, thank you,**
For forming into life
The thing I cannot yet see.

**Yes, Love, thank you,**
May these four words
Be prayer enough
For today...

4

O Love,
  **Bless the winter waiting**
  With readying stillness
  Awakening awareness
  Of Your bright movement
  Even when night is long
  And cold persists with "no."

**Let no weight of life's winter**
  Keep me from the stretch
  Necessary to offer praise
  Arising from quiet awe
  Of what You secretly form
  Even as the world sleeps.

**Yes, renew in me a courage**
  To stretch toward You
  Even when spring's leaf
  Seems a distant promise
  And even further memory.

**Take this small act of faith**
  And reveal some new light
  Otherwise impossible
  To believe or behold
  Given winter's resistance
  To Your persistent possibilities.

**With the light of Your love**
  Form deep within me
  A posture of prayer
  That stretches my soul
  In the direction of You
  Already rooting me
  In Your soil of "yes"
  In answer to every "no"
  Of winter's weariness.

**By this of You**
  Raise me up again
  And again and again
  In persistent praise
  Of every unseen gift
  You are already forming
  Even in winter's wait.

## Winter's Wait

# Enlarge the Inn

**Loving God**,
Form in me a room
Ever larger for You
As You arrive
In Your thousand disguises
Bearing urgent pregnant hope
Into a world overfull
With desperation and despair
From violence of empires
Too long bearing a scepter
Meant for Your will alone.

**Yes, swing freely the door**
Necessary for more light
To break in with a dawn
Formed by You in answer
To every night's resistance
To Your new day in formation.

**Let this light of You**
Search every corner
In the inn of me
Uncovering hidden things
Too often ignored
In settled comfort
Or distracted by devils of inertia
Too frequently residing
In soul space meant for You.

**By this of You, stretch me**
And open me wide to Your will
Birthing Your Holy Christ
In whatever way You desire
That Your cry of Life
May pierce the night
Turning the heart
Of Your human family
Toward You in awe
In wonder and in praise.

**By this, form Your song**
Of ancient heavenly angels
In this little voice of me
Joining Your chorus
Resisting the lie
Of "not enough room"
Offered by the world
In insult to Your abundant
Space and provision
Always more than enough
In every age and time.

**Yes, O Love of Life**
Swing wide the door
Stretch the inn of my heart
And birth Your Christ-love
Anew in this life of me
For the good of this world
You so dearly love.

*Yes, let it be so, in the inn of me, for Thee.*

BEGINNING ————————————————————

———————————————— AGAIN

**O Love,**
Thank you for the gift
Of beginning again
When all seems lost
Or weariness wears down
The last inch of hope.

**Yes, turn the page**
Of over-rehearsed despair
Or dread of dullness
Formed by too much
Of just about everything.

**Form instead Your promise**
When night's weight
Seems too heavy for
Dawn's readiness to rise
In surprises unlikely
To be noticed by the world
Yet formed by You
As the beginning place
Of Your grand renewal.

**Starting as one small baby**
Still in formation
Not yet ready to be born
You quicken the senses
With miraculous movement.

**Yes, form this advent**
Of Your grand reversal
In me as I wait in wonder
At what You will readily reveal
In this long season
Of late dawn and early dusk.

**Help me savor the beauty**
Of what I do not know
Urging me to wait
When all around me
The world rushes
In frenzy of the overfull,
The too much and the too soon.

**Still me into the gift**
You so yearn to give
Of silence rising
From deep within
Touching everything
With Your cosmic creation
Daring to form a new world
Unknown by the old one
Satisfied with a hypnosis
Of over-rehearsed hopelessness.

**Yes, grant me**
An Advent awakening
Muting every resistance
And releasing a new song
Of thanks for Your grand gift
Of beginning again…
Here…now…yes…thank you.

**O Love, bear in me**
Your surprising blessings
Revealing in every night
Your Holy light.

**Fill the hole in my soul**
With Your heaven of love.

**Hold my weeping and mourning**
In Your healing embrace.

**Release me from myself**
Revealing Your abundance
In everything that rises
From the earth of Your making.

**Form in me a hunger for You**
Filling me with a will and way
Aligned with Your love alone.

**Gift me with mercy**
Bearing new beginnings
For others and myself
Caught in rehearsals of regret.

**Cleanse the lens of my heart**
And reveal Yourself at every turn
This day will necessarily require.

**Press Your precious peace into me**
Formed by Your deep desire
Revealing everyone as beloved
Children born from Your heart.

**Grant me courage and strength**
When persecuted for persistence
In living Your love unflinchingly
That Your reign may rule the day.

**Let no word of resistance to You**
Born out of the world's fear
Be greater than Your gladness
Promised to prophets
And poets who dared to speak
Your word of holy healing
Bearing inside every brokenness
A blessed and new beginning.

**Yes, Love, by this of You**
Birth your joy and gladness
And more than I can name
Readying me to bless
In some small way
This world You so dearly love.

# Surprising Blessings

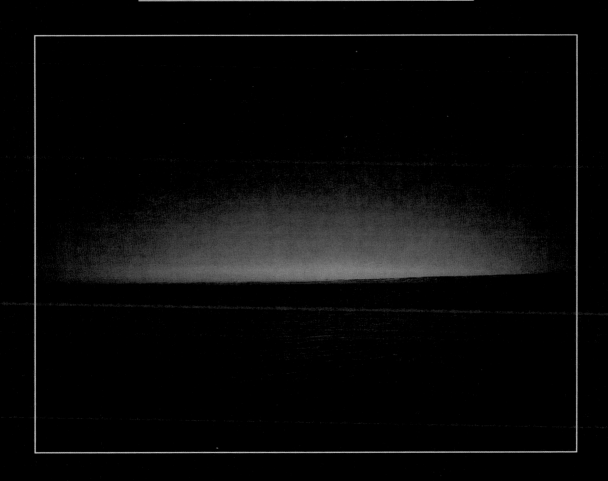

## A Beatitude Prayer

Light

O Love, shine
  Your bright morning star
  And break the night
  Of violence and empire
  And everything resistant
  To Your vision of peace.

Let Your light form hope
  In unlikely places
  Among people weary
  With too much war
  Yearning for another way.

Let it interrupt the inertia
  Of perpetual retribution
  Practiced again and again
  In every age and time
  As the only answer
  To humanity's shared pain.

Instead awaken anew
  Your alternative vision
  Born in babes who cry
  For a new will and way
  To take hold for good.

Let their cries
  And the cries of parents
  Everywhere exhausted
  Be the clarion call
  Interrupting cycles
  Of violence too long
  Practiced as the only option
  In response to unspeakable
  Injury, loss, and death.

Yes, cast Your Holy light
  Of restorative justice-love
  Across the whole creation.

And help the world embark
  On a different journey
  Bearing surprising gifts
  For unlikely recipients
  Born of graces unexplainable
  Except for their power
  To turn the world around
  One act of love at a time.

Let each small act
  Of love-infused gifting
  Empowered by You
  Form a momentum
  For the miraculous
  Otherwise thought impossible
  Except for the Holy interruption
  Of Your saving grace.

Let this work begin anew
  Here and now in me
  And in every human being
  Who yearns for Your newness
  And Holy healing to rise
  In the light of a brand new day.

O Heart of Life,
  Unfold Yourself in me
  Forming a beauty
  Not yet fully seen
  But promised
  With petals dancing
  In delightful anticipation
  Of Your forming grace.

Quiet me
  Into the present miracle
  Of life's emergence
  All around in everyone
  And everything
  Though often hidden
  By hurry or hurt
  In a world weighty
  With too much
  Of things too many
  To name.

Still me, O Love,
  As You rise and unfold
  New vistas of beauty
  Opened in small things
  To reveal Your large love
  And your desire for delight
  To reign against impossible
  Odds of the world's making.

In grand grace,
  Let abundance form
  From Your heart center
  In anticipation of days
  Not yet ready to receive
  The hidden beauty
  You store in every seed
  For just the right time
  Of sacred emergence
  Combining root and stem
  Into flowering fragrance
  Bearing life for busy bees
  Of all shapes and sizes.

But for now,
  Let me delight
  In today's gift of beauty
  Freely given to inspire
  And open the heart
  Of this life of me
  Birthed to praise You
  By awakening others
  To the beautiful blossom
  You are opening in them.

**Blossoming Heart**

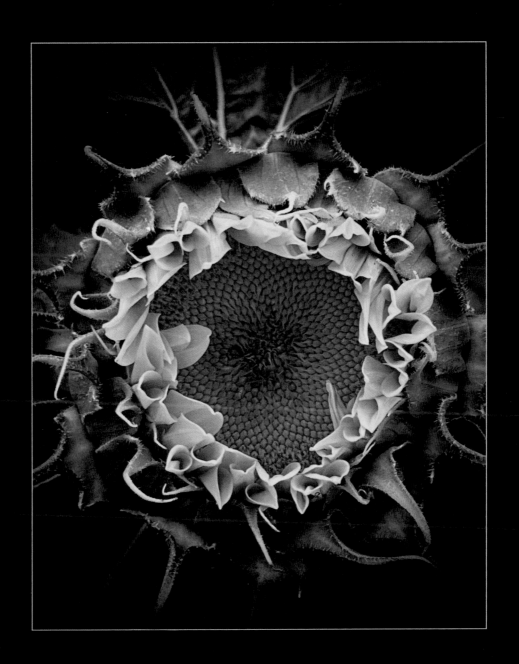

Loving Presence,
  Anchor me
  For seas around and within
  Often sweep me off course
  In violation of my best intentions
  To follow Your North Star
  Leading to the true shore
  Of my deepest longing.

Yes, be my sea anchor
  Bearing your deep stillness
  Amid tidal waves of noise
  Easily drenching despair
  In perpetual soak of cynicism
  In a world gone mad with
  Warmongering and fear.

Let Christ's interrupting
  Command to "Be still"
  Be my ready anchor
  For whatever storms
  May rise within me
  Or arrive on winds of worry
  Stirred by forces beyond.

Let no momentary whirlwind
  Be stronger than your anchor
  Of lavish love
  Tender mercy
  Gentle grace
  And everlasting joy.

Tether me to this
  Of Your deep desire
  And perpetual promise
  That I may be strengthened
  For whatever storm
  Tempts me to come undone
  From the anchor of You.

Yes, Holy One
  Anchor me
  Always, again, in You.

## Sea Anchor

## Precious

O Love,
Already You awaken me
Your Precious Presence
A pausing chapel of silence
Holding everything
In every moment of now.

Help me savor
This gift You offer
Shaping and renewing
In constant evolution
Often hidden by urgencies
Arranged by a world
Gone mad with hurry.

Yes, Love,
Still me again and again
Into the mystery of You
Yearning for my return
From every detour
To distant lands
Of my misplaced longing.

Lure me, O Holy One,
Forming a hunger for You
Stronger than any other
Calling me to the deeper joy
Of Your delightful desire
Joining the whole creation.

Grant me the grace
Of liminal space
Revealing the horizon
Of Your love alone.

Let Your bread of heaven
Feed me to fullness
Not of my making
But received as gift
Even as You call me
To share the bread of earth.

Yes, Love,
Grant me the grace
Of a sacrament such as this
Feeding the world
As You feed me
With Your precious presence.

## Presence

O Love,
Press Your joy
Into the prickly place
Arising from deserts
Of discouragement
Too deep to name.

Let no sting of death
In the present moment
Be greater than the promise
You revealed in Jesus
Giving persistent rise of life
Through unlikely people
From out of the way places.

Yes, bring forth
Some unexpected fruit of joy
From every desert of despair
Seemingly dead at first sight
Yet bearing possibilities
Born from Your creative heart.

May the light of your love
Land everywhere on everyone
And bring forth a bloom
Bearing breathtaking beauty
Otherwise unimaginable
In the desert place.

By this, of You,
Form Your Holy joy
Even as the necessary work
Of building beloved community
Continues its urgent march
In a world often paralyzed
And prickled with pain.

Yes, even here
Especially here
In the prickly place
Of desert's making
Water Your world
With Christ-grace
And gift Your whole creation
With just enough root
For Your joy to rise.

## Desert Joy

# HOLY ONE,

### Reorder my life
With Your piercing love
And cut away every growth
That chokes the breath You give.

### Reorder my thinking
Giving first place to You,
Too often an afterthought,
If even any thought at all.

### Reorder my heart
Too often consumed
With blinding selfishness
Preventing me from seeing
The gift of You in others
Beautiful and already present.

### Reorder my desires
Into the One desire
Given as command
But truly offered as a plea
To unlock every door
Of heart and mind
With the Love You are
O Way, O Truth, O Life.

A LIFE

REORDERED

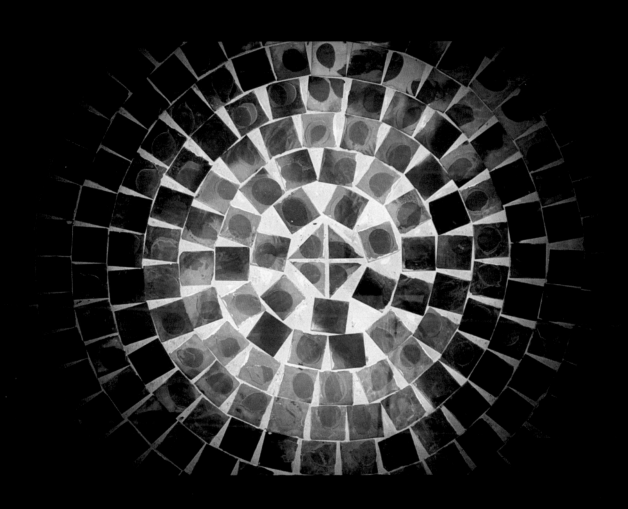

# Necessary Sabbath Rest

**O Love,**
Grant me grace
To receive Your Sabbath
Rest and renewal
So often resisted
In frenzied rush
Toward inertias
Of my own making.

**Let breathing space**
Awaken me to Your breath
Given as gift in every moment
For a soul sustenance
Often taken for granted
Yet bearing the miracle of life
Into my body, mind, and spirit.

**Let sacred pause still me**
Into awe and wonder
At mysteries little and large
Too often taken for granted
By a heart and mind overfull
With distractions dividing
My attention at every turn.

**Settle me enough**
To notice Your precious pulse
Pressing Your life through me
And in others around me
Permeating Your whole creation
Already singing a song of praise
If only I will stop and listen
To the birdsong of early spring.

**Yes, let your Sabbath gift**
Bear me up in light and love
And offer rest from my restlessness
In discovery of Your resurrection
Already bearing its eternal motion
In this body of me and the world.

**Here…now…yes…**
        **thank you…O Love.**

O Love,
   Stretch my life
   In praise of You
   Bearing up from wilderness
   Soil of rocks and sand
   A posture of praise
   For all You make possible.

Let no desert time
   Prevent a holy pause
   In awe of Your display
   Of purple mountain
   Majesty and mystery.

Grant me grace
   In the desert place
   To discover a beauty
   Otherwise thought impossible
   Save for the gift
   Your loving light reveals
   In places unlikely
   And often unwanted.

Stir me to wonder
   At Your desire to reveal
   Your resilient will and way
   In spaces and times
   Easily dismissed as unable
   To bear anything fruitful.

Yes, capture my attention
   In this space of life
   I would otherwise ignore
   In temptation to search
   For the familiar
   Or more favorable.

Instead root me deep
   In Your desert soil
   Reaching and readying me
   For Your water of Life
   To rise up in support
   Of the posture of praise
   You have birthed me
   To prayerfully pose.

# A Sign

**O Love,**
Stretch Your promise
Over every hard place
Calling forth hope
Pulling me on Your path
To destinations unknown
Except by You, O Source
And goal of Love and Life.

**Grant me grace**
To lift my eyes
From daily drudgeries
Toward awesome sights
Inspiring every slow step
On the long journey
Toward justice, peace,
And earth's full flourishing.

**Yes, pause me into the gift**
Cast large by You
Bending beauty and hope
Toward a humanity hardened
By too little vision
Of Your sacred offering
Pressed from Your heaven
Of love and grace
Into the heart of life.

**Let this promised bow**
Be enough reminder
Of Your renewing grace
For today's challenges
Little and large
Filled with longing
For the something more
You constantly offer
If I will raise my eyes
And open my heart to You.

**Yes, Love,**
Bend Your beauty
Over the road of today
And bear up the world
For every unexpected
Detour this day reveals.

**And let it be**
More than enough
For each next step
On this sacred journey
Toward Your promised joy.

of Promise

## RISING UP

O Love of Life,

Let all my noticing
 Arise from You
Let all my hope
 Arise from You
Let all my wonder
 Arise from You
Let all my delight
 Arise from You
Let all my gratefulness
 Arise from You
Let all my words
 Arise from You
Let all my work
 Arise from You
Let all my passion
 Arise from You
Let all my peace
 Arise from You
Let all my joy
 Arise from You
Let all my desire
 Arise from You
Let all my love
 Arise from You.

For no good thing
 No worthwhile dream
 Can ever flourish
 Apart from rising up
 In, from, and through You,

O Love of Life.

**Loving God,**
When devils in disguise
Threaten to unhinge my life
Grant me a grit of grace
Transforming temptations
Into opportunities to grow.

**Deepen my desire for You**
Instead of the sneaky things
So easily demanding attention
Dressed up in pre-occupations
Too numerous to count
Their constant flow daring me
To give my heart and soul away
In worship of lesser things.

**Grant me a strength of spirit**
Larger than my own ability
Yet using every gift You give
To grow through the resistance
Necessary for a healthy heart
To be readied for Your flow
Of love into the world in words
And deeds yet to be revealed
In this gift of one more day
Given by You for love's unfolding.

**UNHINGED**

**Help me remember to call on You**
At temptation's every turn
Daring me to distraction
Luring me with unsatisfactory
Siren songs calling out
For embrace of my lesser self
Easily exchanging Your gift
For some soul-narrowing inertia.

**When I discover myself unhinged**
Grant me also the gift
Of remembering Your grace
To begin again and again
Running home to Your embrace
Trusting each new beginning
Will strengthen me just enough
To discover my soul stretched
By Your constantly loving Spirit.

**By this, grow in me a strength**
To do the hard things of today
Empowered by Your Christ-love
That I may be grown by You
In whatever way You desire
Reattached to Your Holy will
As You rehang the door of my life
And swing me open to love others
Also likely unhinged along the way.

34

Today, O Love,
Let there be a rising
Of joy-filled justice
Holy hope and daring delight
At the gift of all things good.

Yes, let the bird of spring
Be a sign of promise
Awakening me to You
And all you make possible
When the wing of the heart
Is stretched into soul space
Formed by You before time
Tried to hold all hope hostage.

Help me spread the wings
Of a life often grounded
By fatigue or forgetfulness
Into a posture of praise
Giving space to rise
As your Spirit lifts.

Radiate a hope
For unexpected risings
Answering winter's lingering
With a spring of anticipation
Offering new perspectives
Brightened by Your holy gift
Landing without exception
On everyone and everything.

O Love,
Grant again the gift
Of Your soaring spirit
Able to lift out of despair
Every heaviness of heart
Into delightful discovery
Of your Light of Love.

Spirit

Soaring

# Becoming

**O Love,**
Thank you for silence
Rising, resting, holding
Heart, mind, and body
In sacred submersion
Of Spirit beyond my knowing
But through which I am known.

**Gift descending or arising**
I know not how or why
Only that eternity visits
In the precious gift of now.

**Let me receive it**
Not trying to figure it out
As if created by me
In some laboratory of ego
Aching to be noticed
As guard against the unknowing
Necessary to be formed
By You, O Love, who is Life.

**Yes, Love,**
Let me receive the gift
You yearn to offer
Unmade by me
Yet making me
If I will surrender
My will to You
Into the precious
Presence You are
And are always
**Becoming . . .**

# TURNING TOWARD AWE

O Love,
  Keep turning me toward You
  When the god of negativity
  Would tempt me to worship
  At the altar of despair.

Break its grip on my attention
  Granting grace to step back
  From my preoccupations
  And awaken me to all
  That is beautiful and true and good.

Grant me grace toward myself
  That I may extend it to others
  Not in denial of my need to grow
  But as the necessary ground
  For every good thing to rise.

Let me praise You
  In word and song and silence
  For the gift of this day
  And every moment in it
  As the opportunity it is
  To pause, savor, give thanks
  And extend this wonder
  You constantly place before me
  Fashioning a new creation
  Out of what seems a dead end.

Yes, Love,
  Grant the grace of awe
  In the simplest of things
  That I may be readied
  For wonder at mysteries large
  Already holding me
  Patiently awaiting my discovery.

# O Love,

Birth me anew...again...from above...

**Let Your Blessed Silence,**
Still me into You
That I may trust
Your forming grace
Sorting and strengthening
Especially the littlest things
Often the foundation
Of larger things
Only revealed in a time
Not of my making
Nor measurable by me.

**Let extraordinary ordinaries**
And newfound blossoms
Awaken me to the miracle
Of Your persistent aliveness
Unfolding the grand mystery
Of Your ever-new creation
Using every challenge
To build a strength of soul
Formed by Your love alone
For love of You alone
Arriving in Your many disguises.

# REBORN

**Form every ordinary thing**
Into a prayer that opens
My heart again and again
To Your surprising presence
Pausing me into the Holy
You delight to readily reveal
If I will simply stop and savor
The simplest of things
Revealed in Your Holy silence.

**Yes, Blessed Spirit,**
Pour Yourself ever anew
Clarifying and cleansing
Healing and holding
My very human heart
For this of your revealing
Moment to moment
Hour to hour
And day to day.

# Love

All Life is permeated by Love...

**D**

**A**

**I**

**L**

**Y**

**O** Love,
Baptize me anew
With an outpouring
Of Your cleansing Spirit
Renewing me inside
For the outer life
You call forth today.

**G**round my thinking
My praying, my hoping
My everything in You;
Make clear my intentions
Make pure my actions
Make graceful my words
Make hopeful my heart.

**G**ift me with challenges
Necessary for my growth
That I may love You
And Your beloved creation
More wholly and more fully.

**B**

**A**

**P**

**T**

**I**

**S**

**M**

**E**specially help me savor
The beloved identity
Of the "other" I encounter
In whatever form You reveal
Calling to me from them
In order for me to know
You in Your infinite variety
More thoroughly and deeply.

**Y**es, grant me wonder
At your awesome arrival
Honoring the Christ You reveal
In otherwise ordinary encounters
Always filled with Holiness
Forming a hidden wholeness
So often obscured by my fear
Or that of the world's making.

**Y**es, Love,
Baptize me in Your Spirit
And form me anew
In the gift of this day
For whatever You desire.

## Holy

O Eternity of Grace,
  Pause me into the mystery
  Of a life scooped up
  From ashes of yesteryear
  Into a body breathed
  By You for a time
  Not of my making.

Form in me a reverence
  For all You re-member
  In Your creation from dust
  Bearing up every living being
  Carrying Your imprint
  Of holiness for a time.

Yes, let Your Holy miracle
  Not escape my notice
  In pursuit of other things
  Often pressing me to ignore
  Your ever-present presence
  Forming life from death
  And returning it to earth
  In due season of Your design.

Today let Your Holy sign
  Of ash-formed cross
  Be my constant reminder
  Of this gift of life You give
  Infusing earth with eternity
  Born in infinite variety.

Let it also be a sign
  Worn into the world
  For a wider awakening
  Pausing others in passing
  Into an awareness of Life
  Given freely by You
  In Your persistent raising up
  And laying to rest ashes
  In daily exchange.

Yes, Love, pause me today
  Into this of Your Holy motion
  Holding everything
  In life and death
  And Life beyond death.

## Ashes

47

**O Love,**
Grant grace for this week
Of walking the Holy way
Of remembrance and risk
Of riot and resurrection.

**Help me to release**
My present and future
Into Your loving embrace
Not knowing where the road
Of Your renewal may lead.

## FOR EVERY WEEK HOLY

**Form the heart and mind**
Of Christ in me
In daring commitment
To your will and way of love
No matter the twists and turns
Of rough roads trod
Or the vitriol of voices encountered.

**Let me die to all the detours**
Of my own design and distraction
Trusting You will hold me
In life and death
And life beyond death
No matter the pressure
Or pain of the present moment.

**Let no resistance**
To Your love within or beyond
Be greater than the grace
And strength of Christ
Whose Jerusalem journey
Already reveals Your power
In what the world calls weakness.

**At the last, O Love,**
Interrupt again the inertia
Of a world gone mad
With fear and violence
And form instead Your Holy renewal
With resurrection surprises
Too frequent to deny
And too beautiful to ignore.

**Especially grant me strength**
When tempted to run away
From Your demands of love.

**Yes, Love,**
By this week
In this week
For this week
Write my story again
Into Your Holy story
And let it be more than enough.

# THE
# HOLY
# PAUSE
# OF SATURDAY

There is no song but silence
On this sacred Saturday
Holding every yesterday
Whose twists and turns
Reveal a shadow
Lingering even now.

Such Holy waiting
Carries its own hope
Today's pause pressing
A power not yet ready
To be known or heard
By any ordinary way.

Now tomb becomes womb
And all is made in secret
A symphony assembling
While all creation sleeps
Awaiting Light's rising
Striking the downbeat
Of compositions unheard
Until just the right time
Of Love's arrival.

But for now,
The song must wait
And every instrument pause
Readying for the rhythm
Of the Creator's cause.

A Grief

Interrupted

O Love, is it true
**That grief must always win**
Bearing down heavy
In weight of what was
Sucking out life's breath
At every turn of memory?

**Must the upper hand always**
**Be given to grief's will and way**
Bringing tender tears
In relentless remembrances
Sore and sweet all the same
Turning day into night
Resisting sun's reminder
Of new possibilities rising?

**Today, O Love, resurrect me,**
**Saying no to grief's command**
Surprising expected sadness
With unexpected morning light
Tearing open grief's heavy door
Announcing a going forth ahead
Revealing impossible meetings
Made possible by a motion
Only You can breathe to life.

**Now, open the tomb of my heart,**
**Too often pre-occupied**
With death's demands
Disguised as the final word
Unable to see the script
You write even with death
To bring Your good will
And Way of Love to life.

**Let early bird song**
**Be a hallelujah**
Each layer of sun
On ordinary sights
An awakening to You
Who brings this new day
As a gift of "yes"
To persistent "noes"
Commanding attention
Meant for You alone.

**O Holy One who bears**
**Life through death**
In ways improbable
Except for Your Christ-Love
That rises unstoppable
Grant my grief a rest
And enliven me again
With Your rising
New creation in Christ.

# IMPROVISATIONS

**O Love, now**
The Easter journey continues
Through which no experience
Of life is left out...

Hope and hatred
Joy and jealousy
Blessing and betrayal
Desperation and desire
Emptiness and empire
Suffering and silence
Quaking earth
And quiet morning
Tears of sadness
And shouts of gladness.

**You use it all**
In improvisations of grace
Constantly reforming the end
With beginnings unimaginable.

**So help me remember**
Each moment, an Easter journey
If I will but pause and notice
The miracles of Your remaking
In even the smallest of breaths.

**Grant me awe**
At the discovery
Of being born again
In every moment
If I will only notice
The miracle of You
In the strange disguise
Of a gardener...

Or showing up in places
Locked and fearful
Revealing suffering's scars
And their inability to entomb
Your relentless urge of love
Bringing all things into the Life
You are, always have been
And always will be.

**Yes, O Love,**
**You are who You are**
**And so I am alive...**

OF GRACE

**O Love,**
Grant me grace
To trust the gradual
Stretching just enough
To strengthen without injury
But more than inertia desires
In quiet seduction
Toward lesser things
Or a shrinking heart.

**Yes, tune my soul string**
With an increase of love
Steady and willing
To face hard things
And celebrate small victories
Often starting with myself
So often seduced
By unholy attachments
To attitudes or aches
Formed by yesterdays past.

**Reveal to me again**
The gift of the small thing
Done with great love
Invisible to the world
And all it counts as worthy
Yet seen and celebrated
By You who are Love itself.

**Let such little things**
Tune my soul again and again
To Your persistent presence
Penetrating the deep place
You continue to reveal to me
Formed ever deeper by You
In ways beyond my words.

**Help me embrace**
The prayer of playing
Tuning heart and mind
In some grand mystery
Daily releasing beauty
Inspired by you
And urged on by others
Also offering a sacred sound
Of soulful delight into a world
Desperate for such a pause.

**Let this gift you give, O Love,**
Not be taken for granted
Rather received and released
In some grand soul stretching
Bearing Your sacred song
Into the life of the world
One tune at a time.

**Yes, tune my soul**
For this of You in me.

# The Gift of No

**O Love,**
Grant me the gift of "no"
Necessary for yeses
Grounding me again
In the direction
Of Your Holy desire.

**By "no" to myself**
Grow Your freedom
Often held hostage
By my wandering mind
And a wayward heart.

**Gift me with a grace**
To gently pause
Notice, and release
Inertia and entropy's drain
Of my soul's deepest desire
Planted by You, for You
Yet exchanged for momentary
Impulses promising a fullness
Only You alone can provide.

## Yes, Love, still my soul

Into your promised Presence
Beginning with a "no"
To everything that tempts
Me to settle for less
Than all You desire
For my life
And the life of the world.

## Grant me strength

To say "no" to myself
In order to turn
Toward Your promised "yes"
Able to make all things new
Despite every detour
My heart so easily pursues.

By this, grant me
The centeredness of soul
Necessary to be whole.

O Love,
Form in me
A fjord of You
Fashioning a way
Through hard places
Too often worshipped
As holy hills
Insistently resistant
To Your Holy flow.

Yes, let this flow
Of Your eternal love
Awaken me anew
To Your marvelous motion
Drawing me into You
Forming a cavern
Readied for graces
Too deep to name
Yet filling my soul
With overflowing
Abundance and awe.

**F J O R D   O F   L O V E**

Grant me grace
To lovingly trust
Your promised presence
Carving out new creations
From depths unnamable
Yet wholly inhabited
By You, O Living Water
Of Love and Life.

By this of You
Magnify Your beauty
And amaze me again
With Your uncovering
Of Heaven's kiss
Toward earthly things
Revealed in every turn
This day requires.

Yes, form in me
A fjord of You
And let it bear
Some reflection
Of Your beauty
Into the life
Of the world.

**O Love, awaken us**
To the holiness
Of every land
In every time
Bearing layer upon layer
Of peoples who cry
From the earth,
Their stories crushed
By conquest of others
Believing the land
Belonged only to them.

**Interrupt the cycles**
Of persistent delusion
Pretending it is possible
To own the earth
To which we all return.

**Instead raise a reverence**
Not only for the ground
Temporarily standing us up
But also for the people
You scoop into life
In some marvelous motion
Of creative Word and Breath
Indescribable except as miracle.

**Yes, remove our shared madness**
Resisting this truth of You
In careless caricature
Allowing desperate divides
Leading to needless death.

**Bear in us instead**
A new beginning
Born of reverence
For every creature
Birthed by You
From the Holy ground
Of this ball of life
You have cast
Into Your universe
Of creative becoming.

**Stir in us an imagination**
Holy and whole
Layering the land
With Your energies of love
Expressed through every life
You so graciously gift.

**By this, bless the land**
And everyone in it
Recovering its original purpose
To bear a Holy wholeness
Of flourishing joy and delight
For everyone, everywhere,
In every time.

The Body Aches

O Love,
  Let the ache of my body
  Teach me to listen
  To the ache of Your body
  Of people stretched too far
  By needless violence
  Repetitive injury
  And even death.

Teach me the exercise
  Necessary for tending
  The mending of joints
  Torn apart by perpetual
  Inattention to aches
  You give as signs
  Awakening a call
  To move differently
  In the world You love.

Let me love my body's aches
  Enough to awaken me
  To the ache of the world
  Pausing me into exercises
  Of love joining my heart
  To the heart of others
  Through Your heart, O Love.

By this, work your healing
  In me and in the world
  With exercises of love
  Tending the tender place
  Stretching me just enough
  Into Your deep desire
  For strength and growth
  Necessary for mending
  The broken place.

Yes, let no ache
  Of Your body human
  Go untended or ignored
  Languishing in anguish
  For healing and hope
  To rise anew.

O Love,
  Draw your dream
  Deeply in the heart
  Of every human being
  Leaving no one out
  Of the healing hope
  You desire everyone
  To discover.

Pour your Spirit
  Into the soul
  Of the human family
  Drawing it together
  In defiance of divisions
  So easily embraced
  As the new normal.

By Your way of love
  Form a new will
  Within and among
  Every beating heart
  Pulsing everything
  And everyone
  With Your heartbeat
  Of grace and goodwill.

Yes, Love,
  Reform humanity's heart
  To better reflect Your image
  To each other and to ourselves
  Embracing again the high call
  For which we have been birthed
  To love for the good of the other.

By this, of You,
  Form Your new creation
  From exhaustion to energy
  From hatred to healing
  From fear to love
  From despair to delight.

Let Your dream
  Become our highest desire
  Beginning again and again
  For as long as it takes
  That Your joy may rise
  In the human family
  Here and now.

**Formed by**

**Love's Dream**

**O Love**,
Form today's work
Into something holy
Beautiful and good.

Let the buzz of urgency
Be balanced by being
Attentive to the miracle
Of discovering the gift
Of the smallest actions
Bearing life and sweetness
In ways that surprise
And awaken me into awe.

Yes, help me remember
The gift of the small
Seemingly insignificant
Through which You create
The world and me again
And again and again
In constant motion
Of life and death
And life again.

Let no momentary sting
Of disappointment
Or distraction
Or even despair
Keep me from discovering
Your unfolding gracious gift
Providing what is necessary
For Your sweet life to rise.

Yes, lead me to work
Each flower of today
Trusting Your care
For the delicate dance
Between busy-ness and being
Bearing a life-giving nectar
Of hope made possible
By Your love alone.

And may this little buzz
Of today's busy work
Be formed into good
Bearing a gift of delight
That strengthens others
Unknown to me
Yet always beloved by You.

Yes, Love,
Take my busy ness
And balance it with being
As You use me and others
For Your grand unfolding
Of grace and hope and joy
One flower at a time.

And let this be
More than enough
For today.

**O Love, ripen me...**

**Grant me grace to love**
That Your pulse may enliven me.

**Grant me your joining joy**
Answering the fear of the world
With your radiant Spirit.

**Grant me Your peace to share**
In a world aching to rest
From fractious fighting.

**Grant me Your patience**
Grounding my soul in grace
That I may offer the same to others.

**Grant me Your kindness**
For every rough edge revealed
In myself and all your beloved.

**Grant me a generous Spirit**
Trusting Your resource is enough
For the gift of this day You give.

**Grant me a flood of faithfulness**
Filling my heart with resolve
To trust Your power in all things.

**Grant me Your gentleness**
For every hard thing
Daring to evoke anger or fear.

**Grant me self-control**
Freeing me from the prison
I so easily construct
With perpetual distractions
Covering over the gifts
You yearn to give.

**Yes, Love,**
**Grant me grace to grow**
In this sustaining Spirit
That is You in all things
Seen and unseen.

And let it be
More than enough
**For today.**

Spirit Fruit

SHIFTING
    THE PACE
OF LIFE

**O Love,**
Shift the pace of life
For there is a madness
At work in the world
Accelerating at every turn.

**Or is the madness**
Of my own making,
A world constructed
By compulsive cares
Trying to fit the Holy
Into a life lost
In its own designs?

**Is Your pace of Grace**
And all she promises
Already standing
At the door
Of the morning?

**Is the bird**
Outside my window
Actually announcing
That the angel of awe
Has arrived?

**She beckons**
But not by force
She sings
But only in stillness
Does the beauty
Of her song
Hold sway.

**Still, she comes**
And by some grace
Of the morning
In her coming
The cosmos
Pivots from madness
To the marvel
Of Your holy reordering
Called resurrection.

Loving God,
Let every work
Be a labor of love
Built by Your spirit
And giving birth
To precious possibilities
Healing the world's hurts.

Let Life rise in self-giving
Born not of coercion
But freely offered
Answering Your deep call
To discover a life truly alive.

Let no word or act
Be beneath or beyond
Your sacramental search
Forming every ordinary labor
Into a sign holy and healing.

By this let beauty and joy
Blossom bit by bit
Into a world overrun
With weariness and worry.

**EVERY DAY OF LABOR**

Instead let wonder
Open the door of discovery
Awaiting today's effort
Forming every challenge
Into a threshold of holiness
Otherwise seen as obstacle.

O Love,
Let labor and rest
Embrace their delicate dance
Neither always leading
But trading places in trust
Each discovering the need
Of the other's gift and grace.

By this, O Love,
Form the world anew
Rekindling a passion
For Your larger work
Of love's unfolding
Refining everything raw
Into a new creation
Worthy of awe.

O
F

T
H
E

G
R
A
D
U
A
L

O Love,
  Form in me a new season
  Revealing a beauty hidden
  Until the right time
  Fashioning a fire of wisdom
  Fed by yesterday's growth
  When everything was green.

Let me savor and trust
  Your gift of the gradual
  Gently molding my heart
  Draining out every distraction
  Daring to cover Your colors
  Of grace in infinite variety
  Already planted deep within
  Your grand unfolding design.

Help me trust especially
  The gift of aging graces
  Awakening an awe
  Often unrecognized
  In former years of youth
  Now seen at slower pace
  Resisting the world's rush
  Made known in fall's fermata.

Yes, Love,
  Pause me into this
  Of Your revealing grace
  Not knowing how long
  The leaf of this little life
  May hang from the branch
  Awaiting flight to earth's embrace.

Yet even there
  You meet everything
  And everyone in sacred surprise
  Giving birth to beauty again
  In some grand gift of growth
  Formed in Your heart before time
  Or seasons or seconds tried
  To measure Your marvelous mystery.

Form me, O Love,
  With this of You in every pause
  Awakened by your gift of color
  Gradually growing all around.

And let it be enough for today.

O Love,
Grant me grace
To hold tenderly
The breaking open
Of another's life
Revealing mysteries
Otherwise unknown
And often misunderstood.

Let the small opening
Be enough for light
To penetrate depths
Ready to release
Some soul seed
Into the ground
Of Your making.

Give rise to unknown
Fruits of possibility
Unimaginable now
Yet holding a promise
Already known by You
In Your eternity of grace.

B
R
O
K
E
N

O
P
E
N

Yes, Love,
Gift me with gentleness
To hold tenderly
The breaking open
Of another person's heart
Recognizing my own heart's
Necessary breaking
For Your new creation
To rise and release
A beauty not yet seen.

In all of this, grant Your gift
Of the tender embrace
Holding the breaking open
In trust of Your promise
To never leave anyone alone
To face the hard thing
That dares to break
Your unbreakable Spirit
In everything and everyone.

Help me trust
That the breaking open
Is not the end
But only the beginning
For Your good will and way
To reveal itself in all things
That your joy may rise
Ever anew again and again.

## Readying the House

**Loving God, in Jesus**

You emptied
**You turned**
You fed
**You changed**
You healed
**You taught**
You prayed
**You rested**
You wept
**You released**
You forgave
**You washed**
You shared
**You suffered**
You died
**You rose**
You blessed
**You loved**
You sent.

By this of You
**Pour out Your Christ-spirit**
Of resurrection renewal
**And ready again the house**
Of the world and of me
**For Your Holy habitation.**

Thank You

All gratitude
begins and ends
in grace...

**O Love**,
Stretch the human family
With Your Advent promise
Bearing at the end
Some new beginning
Already in formation
Yet not fully in focus
To anyone except You.

**Grant us grace**
To trust Your daily
Evolution of emergence
Bearing possibilities
Known only in slowness
Necessary for growth
At a pace that roots
Deeply your desire
In the soul soil
Of our hardened hearts.

**Yes, penetrate us**
With a hope larger
Than can be seen
In a world practiced
In destruction and death.

**Instead bring forth**
A branch of possibility
Starting surprisingly small
Stopping the madness
Of the world with awe
At Your power of love
To make all things new.

## Advent Stretch

**By this, O Holy Advent One,**
Interrupt violence's voice
Promoting its lie of self-sufficiency
As an adequate narrative
For Your beloved children.

**Let this stretch of You**
Bear its magnificent new song
Here and now, in each of us.

**And join us to the chorus**
Begun with Your Christ-motion
That something of Your hope
May stretch into this old world
And form an ever-new creation.
**Yes, fashion each life**
And that of the world
With an Advent stretch
**And grow us together**
Toward the fullness
Of Your promised peace.

O SNAP

Loving God,
O snap!
**Said too much.**
O snap!
**Said too little.**
O snap!
**Got distracted.**
O snap!
**Overate again.**
O snap!
**Slept too little.**
O snap!
**Veered off course.**
O snap!
**Got cut off.**
O snap!
**Worried all day.**
O snap!
**Plans got changed.**
O snap!
**Tired of waiting.**
O snap!
**Lost my voice.**
O snap!
**Came undone.**

O Love,
**Restring my life**
For some new song
**Tuned with grace by You.**

(And if you can,
Make it just a little bit snappy!)
Thanks for listening.   Amen.

A CONFESSION

**O** Love,
Form Your path in me
Revealing step by step
Your will and way
That leads to awe
And wonder and joy.

**L**et gratitude be my guide
Savoring the little treasures
You place along the way
To pause me into thanks
For the gift of being alive.

**L**et no small thing
Be overlooked in rush
To larger sights begging
Me to move too quickly
Past the present miracle.

**S**till me into a savoring
Of what you reveal
When I embrace the slowness
So often resisted
By my hurried heart.

At the same time
  Help me also notice
  The larger vision unfolding
  Up ahead just a bit
  That stirs my imagination
  Out of any inertia
  Begging me to resist
  Your loving leading.

Yes, grant me the grace
  Of views little and large
  Knowing in both Your gift
  Forming a path in me
  Growing my heart
  Ever-larger in You.

**O Love, form in me**
A thank-you life,
Granting hurry a pause
Long enough to wonder
At your miracles thrown
Right and left at every turn.

**Still me into sacred awe**
Giving thanks for people
Easily taken for granted
Their marvelous presence
So persistent and close
Bearing care and love
For me beyond measure.

**Fashion a thank-you heart**
Expressing in word and deed
Gratitude for the privilege
Of passing on the gift
You give through me to others.

**By this of You**
Lighten my heart
Sometimes heavy
With burdens of my making
Or that of the world's press.

A
T
H
A
N
K

Y
O
U

L
I
F
E

**Let no ugliness or violence**
Of the world's daily design
Crowd out or crush
Your insistent gift
Of resurrection risings
Bearing new beginnings
Often impossible to imagine
If left to human vision alone.

**Break open Your mystery**
Again and again
Answering every breakdown
Of Your human family
With a gift of communion
Formed from ordinary
Elements of abundance.

**Yes, bring to focus the many**
Opportunities for noticing
Your sacred gifts and signs
Scattered across the daily
Path of promise You form
If only I will stop and notice
And offer a simple song
Of thanks and praise.

**Through this of Your revealing**
Form in me a thank-you life
Again and again and again
That Your joy may rise
In the world and in me.

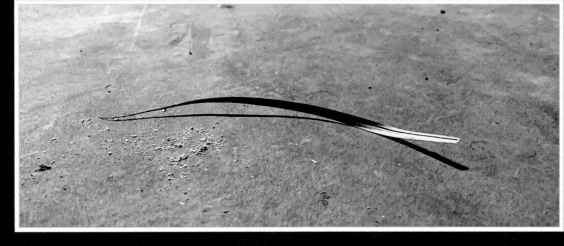

Holy One,
  Bend my life
  With Your arc of love
  Revealing shadows hidden
  An inside I would rather ignore
  Yet necessary to notice
  For Your forming grace
  To fashion me anew
  Again and again.

Let no fear
  Of things hidden
  Keep me from the arc
  By which you bend my life
  Into an emerging creation
  Formed by a love turned
  Toward healing and hope
  No matter the residue
  Of past or present
  Which lies so close.

# Shadow and All

*A Prayer*

**O** Love,
Let even this,
Especially this
Form my heart
With Your silent stretch
Molding every moment
In graces stronger still
Back again to You
Until all is met
In a unity of beauty
Otherwise unknown.

**B**earer of Life,
Let nothing be unused
Shadow nor light
In Your unending urge
By which all things
Are held for healing
Not of my own design
But thankfully formed
By Your Holy grace
Revealing a wholeness
Otherwise unseen.

**Y**es, Holy One,
Bend my life
With Your arc
Of love
Again
And
Again
And
Again…

O Love,
  Slow me into Your sacred
  Revelation of the simple
  Bearing Your presence
  Often overlooked by me
  In rush to accomplish
  The next important thing.

By this, form a presence
  Of heart, mind, and soul
  Awakened to Your moves
  Needing little from me
  Except for reverent awe.

Let this invitation You offer
  Of Sabbath renewal and rest
  Alter my pace and view
  Of what is necessary for today.

## Sabbath Moments

### A Prayer

Through Your gentle grace,
  Let wonder rise
  In silence and conversations
  Shared with loved ones
  Who bear Your Spirit
  In beauty beyond description
  If only I will pause enough
  My inner rush to busyness.

May Your prayer
  Where heaven and earth
  Meet in holy embrace
  Become visible to me
  Through revelations only known
  In the space of soul You form.

Yes, sabbath-soaking Love,
  Open me to Your stillness
  Forming a sacred space
  Of holy anticipation
  That awaits my slowing
  More deeply into You.

Ordinary
Little
Things

**O Love,**
Awaken me to the gift
Of ordinary little things.

**The taste of foods**
Sacramentally soaked
For an awakening
Dance of delight
On a tongue often occupied
With too much speech.

**The feel of breath**
Moving in and out
Gift to a body
I did not make.

**The flower that persists**
Even as snow flies
Daring to cover
The joy it offers.

**The wonder of children**
Helping me see anew
Noticing things long lost
In my taken-for-granted world.

**The unexpected call**
From a friend too long
Silenced by seconds
Strangely become years.

**The kindness of strangers**
Whose door opening
Fashions a flash of connection.

**The red light that pauses**
My hurried journey
Too often missing
Your rising in everything
And everyone all around
Revealing miracles close
Yet often distanced
By needless worry.

**Yes, Love,**
Grant me the grace
Of a grateful heart
Awakened and conscious
Of your persistent gift
Pressing Your presence
Tending the little things
Shaping larger things
With Your Holy motion of love.

**And may the joy you offer**
And the joy I desire
Become one
Little by little
Bit by bit
Yes, Love, thank You.

O Love, thank you
For Your joining joy
Miraculously multiplying strength
Through connection to others
In discovery of solidarity
Larger than the sum
Of the visible parts.

Yes, thank you
For the root that holds
As branches stretch
In some morning praise
Of all You make possible
In ever passing season.

Remind me of the gift
Of offering shade
To others needing rest
From weariness of flight
In search of nesting places
Bearing the possibility
Of new beginnings
Otherwise unimaginable.

Yes, stretch my life
Toward the gift You give
Of others growing near
Also yearning to give
The gift of life outstretched
In mystery of growth.

Root me and grow me
Toward this blessing
You provide in promise
Of a joy only revealed
By savoring the truth
Of being already joined
Root and branch to others
In love, for love
By You, O Love.

**THE NECESSARY FALL**

O Love,
Help me savor the season
Of foliage falling all around
Bearing beauty in dying
Slowly turning the green
Into yellow, red, and orange
A holy fire of sense and spirit.

Let it pause me into wonder
At cycles revealing life large
An outer and inner motion
Bearing birth and death
In constant conversation
Necessary for revelation
Of Your loving longing.

Grant grace upon grace
Meditating on this motion
Of holding and releasing
Of tearing and mending
Of resting and waking
Of dying and rising,
Trusting Your embrace
Holding everything
And everyone all the same
Losing no thing and no one
In Your eternity of grace.

So let every falling leaf
Be a meditation in motion
Descending to the depths
In order to rise again
Transformed into beauty
Not yet conceived
Yet already awaiting
A birth timed by You
O timeless One.

O Love,
  Tend the wound
  Carried within
  Bearing a brokenness
  Held too long.

Rearrange the residue
  Daring to claim
  The final chapter
  Of a story beginning
  And ending in You alone.

Let Your light shine
  A ray of hope
  Into the depths
  Long thought
  Impossible to heal.

By Your Spirit
  Bind up the fragments
  Held invisibly deep
  And form them
  Into a new creation
  Bearing a beauty
  Unbelievable
  Save for the grace
  You revealed in Christ.

Yes, let this wound
  Become an opening
  For a resurrection
  Unimaginable
  Yet already forming
  With Your outpouring
  Of soul-soaking Spirit
  Birthing a blessing
  Unseen by the eye
  Yet readily revealed
  By You in sacred silence.

**TENDING THE WOUND**

Grant me grace, O Love,
  To savor the gift of today
  And grow in me
  Your resilience.

Help me savor the rising
  To early morning's bird song
  And stretch of sunrise
  Bearing gradual light
  Kissing the night goodbye
  In thanks for rest
  Offered to all creation
  Forming dreams mysterious
  Necessary for renewal
  Of body, mind, and spirit.

Help me savor the quiet
  Of a chapel unnameable
  Formed by You deep within
  Stilling my mind
  And reordering my heart
  Breath by breath
  Bearing ever-new life.

Help me savor the exercise
  Of body, mind, and heart
  In thankful joy for pressure
  Just enough for growth
  But not too much to crush
  As world's weightiness
  Is often want to do.

**SAVORING**

Help me savor the learning
  From books and friends
  And strangers unknown
  Whose paths will cross mine
  At just the right moment
  For openings I cannot imagine
  Carrying wisdom from You
  For unexpected growth in me.

Help me savor the beauty
  You lavishly throw around
  Landing everywhere eye turns
  In beckoning abundance
  Calling out for notice
  And worshipful praise
  At all You give and make
  Possible through evolutions
  Of the marriage of life and death
  In constant cosmic creation
  Never finally losing anything
  Or anyone in Your grand unfolding.

Yes, Love,
  Despite every challenge
  And word resistant to You
  In a world gone mad
  In a thousand ways,
  Grow Your resilience in me.

Help me savor the gift
  You give of this precious day.

O Love,
 Gift me today
 With Your Holy interruption
 Slowing my rush
 Into sacred pauses
 Giving way to others
 Intersecting my path
 With a pace that slows
 Me into grateful wonder.

By this of You, restore me
 Gathering every fragment
 Lost in the sprint
 Toward too many things
 Clamoring for my worship
 Tempting me toward illusions
 Of self sufficiencies
 Giving little notice of You.

Yes, Love, interrupt me
 And awaken me to the gift
 Of Your guiding grace
 Always available
 If only I will savor
 The unexpected intersection
 With others bearing a slower pace
 Resisting the world's unholy hurry.

By this, help me discover
 Your ever-new breath
 Bearing Life moment to moment
 Through a precious grace
 Offering everything necessary
 Through Your persistent miracle
 Pressing Yourself into the heart
 Of every living being.

Yes, help me today
 To notice this gift You give
 Especially in interruptions
 Re-arranging my plans
 In  order to open my eyes,
 My mind, and my heart
 To Your Holy revelation
 Brought close in the ordinary.

Through such interruptions
 Renew and restore
 My often scattered soul
 And bear in me a new beginning
 Born of Your life-giving love
 Again and again and again.

O Love,
Help me trust
Your ridiculous abundance
Scattering itself abroad
In reckless abandon
Carried by a wind of spirit
Caring nothing for boundaries
Set by human standards
Of who deserves what
Or when or why or how.

Yes, release me
From every clenching
Of generosities intended
To be shared in delight
For blossoming in places
Unlikely and surprising
Giving pause to resistance
So often ignoring You
And your delightful whimsy.

Draw me anew into this
Of Your scattering grace
Disguised as annoyance
Yet giving rise to color
Catching the eye
In some strange revelry
Of praise and thanksgiving.

O Love, help me live
In anticipation of You
Rising up like this
In Your many disguises
Turning my frustration
Into frolicking joy
Often overlooked
Except by children
Who join in blowing
Your seed all around
With the breath of Life
You give to each
And every one.

Daily
_____

_____

Horizons

O Love,
  Help me remember,
  As the earth revolves
  Around sun's light
  Bathed in energies
  Giving forth life
  So, too, my soul
  Revolves round You
  Who breathes all life
  And lights my way.

Set my soul to succumb
  To this pull of You
  In me and everyone
  And every created thing
  All alive in response
  To Your gravity of grace.

Let this truth descend
  From head into heart
  And form me anew
  In this chapel You make
  For perpetual renewal
  Formed by the daily gift
  Of rising and setting
  Like sun's saturating strength
  On earth's eager horizon.

Yes, Love, help me savor
  The rising and setting
  Of Your radiant Love
  On the horizon of my life
  Seen only as You shine
  Your Spirit across everything
  Seen and unseen by my eye
  Yet wholly envisioned by You.

Let morning's light awaken
  Me to this of You
  Kindling a fire of soul
  For every demand of the day
  Granting perpetual thanks
  For Your bright awakening
  Evoking awe and wonder
  Given as gift
  Not of my making.

Then let awe continue
  At night's arrival
  Savoring rest's gift
  Granting deep renewal
  Growing your dream
  Inside my own
  Given as blessing to me
  By You who dreamed
  Before time began.

Yes, Love,
  Let my life revolve
  Around Your emerging light
  And by it evolve this life
  You give to every living being.

112

FROM
WHICH
THE
BODY
RISES

Holy One,
Let me love Your creation
Not as object to be used
As careless throw-away
But as the womb of life
From which every body rises.

Let no river go unnoticed
Falling victim to actions upstream
With downstream consequence
Too often visited on the vulnerable.

Let every molecule of air
Be honored for the life it carries
In constant exchange
From one body to another
Binding all in indivisible necessity.

Let eating again be sacrament
Savoring every energy
You provide as abundant answer
To every lie of scarcity
Forming fear's fertile ground.

Yes, Love,
Let today's precious pauses
Be prayers of wonder
Cultivating the ground within
And honoring the ground all around
As the Holy place of Your creation
From which every body rises.

AN
EARTH
DAY
PRAYER

O Love,
    Descend lightly as snow
    Dampening the noise
    Of heart and mind
    Easily distracting me
    From the grace
    You scatter everywhere
    On everyone aware or not
    Of Your continual coming.

Mute my voice enough
    Granting space
    For Your silent song
    Word beyond words
    To descend deep into my heart
    Awed by Your ineffable silence.

Let it be the silence
    Of new-fallen snow
    Pausing every ordinary
    Sound of the daily
    Into discovery of the deep
    Life You are in all things.

Set my heart to savor
    This silent deep of You
    Forming in me a solitude
    Giving birth to the words
    You most need and desire
    To be uttered in a world
    Overrun with rumor and rancor
    Drowning out the Life
    You are always yearning
    To offer and reveal.

Especially quiet my ego
    So active and eager
    To prove ridiculous things
    Droning on in endless worry
    Missing Your perpetual promise
    In breaths not of my making
    Yet remaking me constantly.

Pause me into this gift
    To simply say, "Thank you"
    As You remake me
    And Your whole creation
    Softened by the spirit
    You send so freely
    As new-fallen snow.

Precious possibilities
Releasing seeds
Of new beginnings.

**Yes, remake the world**
By planting this motion
Of You deep within
The soil of the human heart.

**By this of You, move us**
From suspicion to love
From anger to awe
From hatred to healing
From fear to understanding
From judgment to joy.

**Yes, break down**
Every barrier
By breaking open
Our closed minds
Our clenched hearts
Our clutched souls
All too tightly wound
Around rehearsals
Of past hurt and pain.

## Holy Healing

Exchange

**Instead awaken us**
  With Your indivisible
  Ever-present connection
  To each other
  Often covered over
  By incessant repetition
  Of retribution and rage
  Too long repeated
  In spirals of grief
  And despair.

**Interrupt our tragic refusal**
  To embrace alternatives
  Persistently offered by You
  If we will risk forgiveness
  That turns a cheek
  And walks a second mile
  In the shoes of another.

**Today, cultivate this courage**
  In even the smallest ways
  Opening our hearts and minds
  So often paralyzed
  With the practice of fear.

**Grant every necessary strength**
  For this of You to rise
  In the heart of humanity
  Forming your ever-new
  Creation of compassion
  Justice, peace, and joy.

**Yes, form us anew**
  With Your Holy exchange
  That we may release
  The shell of yesterday
  And receive Your sacred seed
  Bearing the possibility
  Of a precious peace
  Otherwise unknown
  Save for Your gift of grace.

**O Love,**
Help me savor
The beautiful darkness
Bearing life unseen
Forming in places
Not yet ready
For the day
Of resurrection's rising.

**Let Your large silence**
Hold my words and worries
Enough for me to be freed
From frenzied fear of unknown
Mysteries bearing something
Beautiful beneath the surface
Of sights easily seen in daylight.

**Cultivate the cavern of my soul**
Sorting out every chaos
Held too tight and too close
Too much of the time
And loosen the ground
For Your seed of Spirit
To rise in some new creation
I cannot imagine on my own.

**Gift me with patience**
For this necessary slow work
Fashioned by Your persistent
Waves of love soaking my heart
In dark night's deep
Insisting that something new
Be formed while my body
Mind and soul are held
In necessary rest.

**Yes, help me trust**
Your beautiful darkness
Awakening me to mysteries
Otherwise unknown by me
In the bright light of day
Yet always known
And held by You
Even in soul's dark night.

A Beautiful Darkness

Holy One,
Let your renewing Love
Rise in the impossible
Ways You always have
Using yesterday's quake
As today's new ground
Of beginnings unimaginable
Except in Your Holy heart
Forming life at every turn.

Yes, Love,
Press life from earth's swirl
Otherwise crushing everything
In hot and heavy flow
Of hatred's daring to cover
Your desire for flourishing.

**E**specially, O Love,
  Grant growth in me
   From every hardened ground
   Formed by forces ancient
   Pressing down my heart
    In residue of every yesterday's
    Quake of heart and mind.

   **L**et Your urge
    For new beginnings
    Form itself in spaces
    Unnoticed in my heart
     Except in early morning's
     Invitation to pause in awe
     At this work You already do
     In everything all around me.

    **Y**es, Holy One,
     Cover me over
     With Your lava of love
     Giving rise to impossible
      Growth on yesterday's edges
      For today's beautiful blossoming.

## A Prayer for Renewal

# Temple

O Love,
Bless this temple body
Given as gift by You
Enlivened by Your Spirit
For worship and work
In thanks and praise
Of all You make possible.

Form in me a reverence
For care of this gift
Of body given by You
For the purposes of love
To build Your justice joy
For the full flourishing
Of everybody's body.

Bless my ordinary eating
With your Holy Spirit
And awaken me
To Your precious presence
Bearing Your energy
Of eternity here and now.

Grant me grace
To savor the sacramental sip
Of Your life-giving water
Forming and reforming
Each cell of the universe
Of universes you form
In every living body.

Quiet my mind and heart
Enough to hear Your pulse
Bearing Your life large
In this little body of me.

And let this pulse of You
Grow in me
A loving gratitude
For this temple body,
That I may walk and work
Speak and keep silence
And honor this gift
Given for reverencing
Every body formed by You.

# Body

**Loving God,**
Today, help me savor
Your beautiful unfolding
Scattered at every turn.

**Help me trust**
This emerging motion of You
At work in those around me
And even at work in me.

**Especially grant me grace**
To notice this of You
Emerging in others
With whom I disagree.

**By this, join me**
To Your healing love
Able to see a beauty
Often buried in the seed
Awaiting discovery.

**Grant me enough awe**
To pause my ego
Into discovery of You
Bearing possibilities
I cannot imagine on my own.

**Yes, form Your unfolding**
Motion of gracious love
In the simplest of words
At each turn of today.

**By this, grant a grace**
That lifts the world
Often weighed down
With too much heaviness.

**Today, bend it and me**
Toward Your life-giving
Vision of what is possible
When turned toward You
And Your beautiful unfolding.

# Lectio Divina

# Lectio Divina - An ancient way of praying with scripture

**Prepare (Silencio):** Take a few moments to quiet yourself, get in a comfortable position, and become aware of God's presence of Love. You might say a simple prayer to evoke your awareness of the already present Presence of Love. Sometimes simply becoming aware of your breathing may be prayer enough. You might take a quick inventory of your body, mind, and heart, asking Holy Love to quiet each of them in turn.

**Read (Lectio):** Choose a brief passage of scripture and read it slowly, out loud if possible. Avoid analyzing. Simply savor the words, letting them sink in to your heart. Listen for a nudge. Notice toward what words or images the Spirit is drawing you.

**Meditate (Meditatio):** Re-read the passage, lingering over the person/word/phrase that captured your attention. Let your imagination engage the story/text. What do the characters experience/feel/think? Or consider the phrase or image you noticed: Reflect on how it might intersect with your life today. What (or who) does it bring to your mind? Notice the feelings this passage evokes in you – is there attraction, or resistance of some kind? Invite the Spirit to reveal how this passage might be speaking to your life. You might find it helpful to journal some of these reflections before continuing.

**Pray (Oratio):** Read through the passage another time, allowing the scripture to lead you into a prayer or other response to Love. Talk to the Holy One about what has come to mind and how Love might be inviting you to respond. Are you feeling led toward a prayer of praise? Repentance? A plea for help or healing? Again, it might be helpful to focus your prayer by journaling.

**Contemplate (Contemplatio):** Rest in the awareness of Love's presence, remaining open to anything else the Spirit might stir in your heart. If your mind wanders, gently redirect your thoughts toward the One who is Love. You might use a word from the text you have been praying to recenter you. Then simply be still. Expect nothing. Relax in this moment that is deeper than words and simply savor being held in Love's gracious heart.

# Visio Divina

# Visio Divina - A way of praying with images

**Gaze:** Consider the photo before you. Look slowly and thoroughly, noting the colors, textures, objects, people, places, or things. Savor the image for a time. As you feel ready, allow your thoughts to pass by, making space for the inner eye of the heart to open and interact with the image.

**Reflect:** Take a second, deeper look. Rest in the presence of the image. Allow the image to reach beyond the intellect and into an unconscious level. Notice what moves within you. Allow stillness to rise as you consider the image.

**Respond:** Respond to the image with prayer. Did the image remind you of an experience, person, or issue for which you'd like to offer thanksgiving or intercession? Did it open a new awareness, or spark a conviction? Is there a line from the accompanying prayer that especially speaks to you? Pray with that line and allow your own prayer to rise.

**Rest:** Return to sacred stillness as you contemplate the picture. Notice what happens within you without trying to "make something" happen. Simply allow the love of God to enfold you for as long as you need.

# Picture Index

The following index identifies where each picture was taken.
In many ways, these sights have arisen as a gift to me.
I was simply the one to whom they were revealed.
Likely you have had such an experience
begging you to pause and pull
out your phone or other
device to capture
the amazing
gift of

**Love.**

Picture

3
Three Eggs
Perched on Vent
at Home
Delaware, Ohio
May 2020

13
Picture Rocks Trail
Tuscon, Arizona
December 2023

6
Mount Lemon
Road
Tuscon, Arizona
December 2023

16
Greg and Natalie's
Backyard
Minerva Park, Ohio
June 2022

7
Preservation Hall
New Orleans,
Louisiana
May 2019

17
Landed Anchor
Kristiansand,
Norway
July 2023

9
New Ivy
at Home
Delaware, Ohio
December 2021

19
Cliffs of Moher
Liscannor,
County Clare, Ireland
June 2017

12
Seaside Sunrise
Myrtle Beach,
South Carolina
November 2021

21
Redepemtorist
Renewal Center
Tucson, Arizona
December 2023

24
Bird Bath
Delaware,
Ohio
October 2021

33
Karrer Barn
Dublin, Ohio
February 2023

25
Antelope Island
Salt Lake City, Utah
May 2023

36
Gulf of Mexico
Biloxi, Mississippi
March 2022

28
Romero Canyon
Tucson, Arizona
December 2023

38
Iona Abbey
Iona,
Scotland
April 2005

29
Keauhou Trail
Pahoa, Hawaii
May 2022

39
Episcopal Center
Live Oak, Florida
October 2017

32
Home Garden
Delaware, Ohio
June 2021

41
Home Garden
Delaware, Ohio
March 2023

Picture

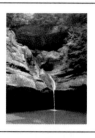

45
Hocking Hills
Old Man's Cave
Logan, Ohio
July 2013

55
River's Edge
Lakewood, Ohio
August 2016

48
Camp Christian
Marysville, Ohio
February 2014

58
J.Kopp Violin
1881
Delaware, Ohio
January 2023

50
Rothenburg
ab der Tauber,
Germany
March 2005

60
Labyrinth
Templed Hills
Bellville, Ohio
April 2021

51
Holy Saturday
Washington, DC
April 2021

61
Gudvangen
Auerlandsfjorden,
Norway
July 2023

53
Barisal,
Bangladesh
February 2020

64
Pine Ridge
Reservation
Shannon County,
South Dakota
July 2018

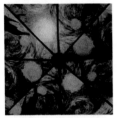

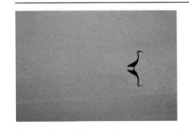

Picture

87
Broken String
at Home
Delware, Ohio
January 2023

97
Breakfast
Blueberries
River's Edge
Lakewood, Ohio
August 2016

90
Pine Ridge
Reservation
Shannon County,
South Dakota
July 2018

100
Trees on Rt. 42
West Jefferson, Ohio
February 2024

91
Commuion Bread
Camp Christian
Marysville, Ohio
October 2023

102
Fall Leaves
at Home
Delaware, Ohio
October 2021

93
Blade of Grass
at Home
Delaware, Ohio
May 2021

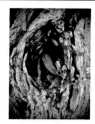

103
Dunkirk
Conference Center
Dunkirk, New York
July 2023

96
Ocean Sunrise
Myrtle Beach,
South Carolina
October 2023

106
Cincinnati Nature
Center
Cincinnati, Ohio
July 2022

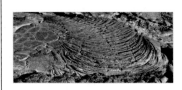

Made in the USA
Monee, IL
10 December 2024

72823988R00095